Baby Shower

In Celebration Of:

_____

Date: _____

Place: _____

baby sprinkle & co.

Find us at Amazon.com/Author/BabySprinkle

Guest

Name & Relationship To The Parents

_____

_____

Message Or Advice For The Parents

_____

_____

_____

_____

_____

_____

Wishes For Baby

_____

_____

_____

_____

_____

_____

Predictions

Date Of Birth: _____

Time Of Birth: _____

Weight: _____

Height: _____

Hair & Eyes: _____

Name: _____

Guest

Name & Relationship To The Parents

_____

_____

Message Or Advice For The Parents

_____

_____

_____

_____

_____

Wishes For Baby

_____

_____

_____

_____

_____

Predictions

Date Of Birth:	Time Of Birth:

Weight:	Height:	Hair & Eyes:	Name:

Guest

Name & Relationship To The Parents

_____

_____

Message Or Advice For The Parents

_____
_____
_____
_____
_____
_____

Wishes For Baby

_____
_____
_____
_____
_____
_____

Predictions

Date Of Birth:	Time Of Birth:

Weight:	Height:	Hair & Eyes:	Name:

Guest

Name & Relationship To The Parents

_____

_____

Message Or Advice For The Parents

_____

_____

_____

_____

_____

_____

Wishes For Baby

_____

_____

_____

_____

_____

_____

Predictions	Date Of Birth:	Time Of Birth:
Weight:	Height:	Hair & Eyes:	Name:

Guest

Name & Relationship To The Parents

_____

_____

Message Or Advice For The Parents

_____
_____
_____
_____
_____

Wishes For Baby

_____
_____
_____
_____
_____

Predictions

Date Of Birth:		Time Of Birth:
Weight:	Height:	Hair & Eyes:	Name:

Guest

Name & Relationship To The Parents

_____

_____

Message Or Advice For The Parents

_____

_____

_____

_____

_____

Wishes For Baby

_____

_____

_____

_____

_____

Predictions

Date Of Birth:	Time Of Birth:

Weight:	Height:	Hair & Eyes:	Name:

Guest

Name & Relationship To The Parents

_____

_____

Message Or Advice For The Parents	Wishes For Baby
_____	_____
_____	_____
_____	_____
_____	_____
_____	_____
_____	_____

Predictions

Date Of Birth: _____

Time Of Birth: _____

Weight: _____

Height: _____

Hair & Eyes: _____

Name: _____

Guest

Name & Relationship To The Parents

_____

_____

Message Or Advice For The Parents

_____

_____

_____

_____

_____

Wishes For Baby

_____

_____

_____

_____

_____

Predictions

	Date Of Birth:	Time Of Birth:
Weight:	Height:	Hair & Eyes:	Name:

Guest

Name & Relationship To The Parents

_____

_____

Message Or Advice For The Parents

_____

_____

_____

_____

_____

_____

Wishes For Baby

_____

_____

_____

_____

_____

_____

Predictions

Date Of Birth:	Time Of Birth:

Weight:	Height:	Hair & Eyes:	Name:

Guest

Name & Relationship To The Parents

_____

_____

Message Or Advice For The Parents

_____

_____

_____

_____

_____

Wishes For Baby

_____

_____

_____

_____

_____

Predictions

Date Of Birth:

Time Of Birth:

Weight:

Height:

Hair & Eyes:

Name:

Guest

Name & Relationship To The Parents

_____

_____

Message Or Advice For The Parents

_____

_____

_____

_____

_____

_____

Wishes For Baby

_____

_____

_____

_____

_____

Predictions

Date Of Birth:

Time Of Birth:

Weight:

Height:

Hair & Eyes:

Name:

Guest

Name & Relationship To The Parents

_____

_____

Message Or Advice For The Parents

_____

_____

_____

_____

_____

_____

Wishes For Baby

_____

_____

_____

_____

_____

_____

Predictions

Date Of Birth:	Time Of Birth:
Weight:	Height:	Hair & Eyes:	Name:

Guest

Name & Relationship To The Parents

_____

_____

Message Or Advice For The Parents

_____

_____

_____

_____

_____

Wishes For Baby

_____

_____

_____

_____

_____

Predictions

Date Of Birth:

Time Of Birth:

Weight:

Height:

Hair & Eyes:

Name:

Guest

Name & Relationship To The Parents

_____

_____

Message Or Advice For The Parents

_____

_____

_____

_____

_____

Wishes For Baby

_____

_____

_____

_____

_____

Predictions

	Date Of Birth:	Time Of Birth:
Weight:	Height:	Hair & Eyes:	Name:

Guest

Name & Relationship To The Parents

_____

_____

Message Or Advice For The Parents

_____

_____

_____

_____

_____

_____

Wishes For Baby

_____

_____

_____

_____

_____

Predictions

Date Of Birth:

Time Of Birth:

Weight:

Height:

Hair & Eyes:

Name:

Guest

Name & Relationship To The Parents

_____

_____

Message Or Advice For The Parents

_____

_____

_____

_____

_____

_____

Wishes For Baby

_____

_____

_____

_____

_____

_____

Predictions

Date Of Birth:	Time Of Birth:

Weight:	Height:	Hair & Eyes:	Name:

Guest

Name & Relationship To The Parents

_____

_____

Message Or Advice For The Parents	Wishes For Baby
_____	_____
_____	_____
_____	_____
_____	_____
_____	_____
_____	_____

Predictions

	Date Of Birth:	Time Of Birth:
Weight:	Height:	Hair & Eyes:	Name:

Guest

Name & Relationship To The Parents

_____

_____

Message Or Advice For The Parents

_____

_____

_____

_____

_____

_____

Wishes For Baby

_____

_____

_____

_____

_____

Predictions

Date Of Birth:

Time Of Birth:

Weight:

Height:

Hair & Eyes:

Name:

Guest

Name & Relationship To The Parents

_____

_____

Message Or Advice For The Parents

_____

_____

_____

_____

_____

_____

Wishes For Baby

_____

_____

_____

_____

_____

_____

Predictions

Date Of Birth:	Time Of Birth:

Weight:	Height:	Hair & Eyes:	Name:

Guest

Name & Relationship To The Parents

_____

_____

Message Or Advice For The Parents

_____

_____

_____

_____

_____

Wishes For Baby

_____

_____

_____

_____

_____

Predictions

Date Of Birth:

Time Of Birth:

Weight:

Height:

Hair & Eyes:

Name:

Guest

Name & Relationship To The Parents

_____

_____

Message Or Advice For The Parents	**Wishes For Baby**

_____   _____

_____   _____

_____   _____

_____   _____

_____   _____

Predictions

Date Of Birth: _____   Time Of Birth: _____

Weight: _____   Height: _____   Hair & Eyes: _____   Name: _____

Guest

Name & Relationship To The Parents

_____

_____

Message Or Advice For The Parents

_____

_____

_____

_____

_____

Wishes For Baby

_____

_____

_____

_____

_____

Predictions

Date Of Birth:	Time Of Birth:

Weight:	Height:	Hair & Eyes:	Name:

Guest

Name & Relationship To The Parents

_____

_____

Message Or Advice For The Parents	Wishes For Baby

_____ _____

_____ _____

_____ _____

_____ _____

_____ _____

_____ _____

Predictions

Date Of Birth:

Time Of Birth:

Weight:

Height:

Hair & Eyes:

Name:

Guest

Name & Relationship To The Parents

_____

_____

Message Or Advice For The Parents

_____

_____

_____

_____

_____

Wishes For Baby ♡

_____

_____

_____

_____

_____

Predictions

Date Of Birth:	Time Of Birth:

Weight:	Height:	Hair & Eyes:	Name:

Guest

Name & Relationship To The Parents

_____

_____

Message Or Advice For The Parents

_____

_____

_____

_____

_____

Wishes For Baby

_____

_____

_____

_____

_____

Predictions

Date Of Birth:	Time Of Birth:

Weight:	Height:	Hair & Eyes:	Name:

Guest

Name & Relationship To The Parents

_____

_____

Message Or Advice For The Parents	Wishes For Baby ♡
_____	_____
_____	_____
_____	_____
_____	_____
_____	_____
_____	_____

Predictions

	Date Of Birth:	Time Of Birth:
Weight:	Height:	Hair & Eyes:	Name:

Guest

Name & Relationship To The Parents

_____

_____

Message Or Advice For The Parents

_____

_____

_____

_____

_____

_____

Wishes For Baby

_____

_____

_____

_____

_____

Predictions

Date Of Birth:	Time Of Birth:

Weight:	Height:	Hair & Eyes:	Name:

Guest

Name & Relationship To The Parents

_____

_____

Message Or Advice For The Parents   **Wishes For Baby**

_____   _____

_____   _____

_____   _____

_____   _____

_____   _____

_____   _____

Predictions | Date Of Birth: | Time Of Birth:
Weight: | Height: | Hair & Eyes: | Name:

Guest

Name & Relationship To The Parents

_____

_____

Message Or Advice For The Parents

_____

_____

_____

_____

_____

Wishes For Baby

_____

_____

_____

_____

_____

Predictions

Date Of Birth:	Time Of Birth:

Weight:	Height:	Hair & Eyes:	Name:

Guest

Name & Relationship To The Parents

_____

_____

Message Or Advice For The Parents

_____

_____

_____

_____

_____

_____

Wishes For Baby ♡

_____

_____

_____

_____

_____

_____

Predictions

Date Of Birth:

Time Of Birth:

Weight:

Height:

Hair & Eyes:

Name:

Guest

Name & Relationship To The Parents

_____

_____

Message Or Advice For The Parents

_____

_____

_____

_____

_____

_____

Wishes For Baby

_____

_____

_____

_____

_____

Predictions

Date Of Birth:

Time Of Birth:

Weight:

Height:

Hair & Eyes:

Name:

Guest

Name & Relationship To The Parents

_____

_____

Message Or Advice For The Parents

_____

_____

_____

_____

_____

_____

Wishes For Baby

_____

_____

_____

_____

_____

_____

Predictions

Date Of Birth: _____

Time Of Birth: _____

Weight: _____

Height: _____

Hair & Eyes: _____

Name: _____

Guest

Name & Relationship To The Parents

_____

_____

Message Or Advice For The Parents

_____

_____

_____

_____

_____

Wishes For Baby

_____

_____

_____

_____

_____

Predictions

Date Of Birth:

Time Of Birth:

Weight:

Height:

Hair & Eyes:

Name:

Guest

Name & Relationship To The Parents

_____

_____

Message Or Advice For The Parents

_____

_____

_____

_____

_____

Wishes For Baby

_____

_____

_____

_____

_____

Predictions

	Date Of Birth:	Time Of Birth:
Weight:	**Height:**	**Hair & Eyes:**	**Name:**

Guest

Name & Relationship To The Parents

_____

_____

Message Or Advice For The Parents

_____

_____

_____

_____

_____

_____

Wishes For Baby

_____

_____

_____

_____

_____

Predictions

Date Of Birth:	Time Of Birth:

Weight:	Height:	Hair & Eyes:	Name:

Guest

Name & Relationship To The Parents

_____

_____

Message Or Advice For The Parents

_____

_____

_____

_____

_____

_____

Wishes For Baby

_____

_____

_____

_____

_____

_____

Predictions

	Date Of Birth:	Time Of Birth:
Weight:	Height:	Hair & Eyes:	Name:

Guest

Name & Relationship To The Parents

_____

_____

Message Or Advice For The Parents	Wishes For Baby
_____	_____
_____	_____
_____	_____
_____	_____
_____	_____

Predictions

Date Of Birth:	Time Of Birth:

Weight:	Height:	Hair & Eyes:	Name:

Guest

Name & Relationship To The Parents

_____

_____

Message Or Advice For The Parents	Wishes For Baby ♡
_____	_____
_____	_____
_____	_____
_____	_____
_____	_____

Predictions

	Date Of Birth:	Time Of Birth:
Weight:	Height:	Hair & Eyes:	Name:

Guest

Name & Relationship To The Parents

_____

_____

Message Or Advice For The Parents

_____

_____

_____

_____

_____

_____

Wishes For Baby

_____

_____

_____

_____

_____

_____

Predictions

Date Of Birth:	Time Of Birth:
Weight:	Height:	Hair & Eyes:	Name:

Guest

Name & Relationship To The Parents

_____

_____

Message Or Advice For The Parents

_____

_____

_____

_____

_____

Wishes For Baby

_____

_____

_____

_____

_____

Predictions

	Date Of Birth:	Time Of Birth:

Weight:	Height:	Hair & Eyes:	Name:

Guest

Name & Relationship To The Parents

_____

_____

Message Or Advice For The Parents

_____

_____

_____

_____

_____

Wishes For Baby

_____

_____

_____

_____

_____

Predictions

Date Of Birth:	Time Of Birth:

Weight:	Height:	Hair & Eyes:	Name:

Guest

Name & Relationship To The Parents

_____

_____

Message Or Advice For The Parents

_____

_____

_____

_____

_____

Wishes For Baby

_____

_____

_____

_____

_____

Predictions

Date Of Birth:	Time Of Birth:

Weight:	Height:	Hair & Eyes:	Name:

Guest

Name & Relationship To The Parents

_____

_____

Message Or Advice For The Parents

_____

_____

_____

_____

_____

_____

Wishes For Baby

_____

_____

_____

_____

_____

Predictions

Date Of Birth:

Time Of Birth:

Weight:

Height:

Hair & Eyes:

Name:

Guest

Name & Relationship To The Parents

_____

_____

Message Or Advice For The Parents

_____
_____
_____
_____
_____

Wishes For Baby

_____
_____
_____
_____
_____

Predictions

Date Of Birth:	Time Of Birth:

Weight:	Height:	Hair & Eyes:	Name:

Guest

Name & Relationship To The Parents

_____

_____

Message Or Advice For The Parents

_____

_____

_____

_____

_____

_____

Wishes For Baby

_____

_____

_____

_____

_____

_____

Predictions

Date Of Birth:	Time Of Birth:

Weight:	Height:	Hair & Eyes:	Name:

Guest

Name & Relationship To The Parents

_____

_____

Message Or Advice For The Parents

_____

_____

_____

_____

_____

_____

Wishes For Baby

_____

_____

_____

_____

_____

_____

Predictions

Date Of Birth:

Time Of Birth:

Weight:

Height:

Hair & Eyes:

Name:

Guest

Name & Relationship To The Parents

_____

_____

Message Or Advice For The Parents

_____

_____

_____

_____

_____

_____

Wishes For Baby

_____

_____

_____

_____

_____

Predictions

Date Of Birth:

Time Of Birth:

Weight:

Height:

Hair & Eyes:

Name:

Guest

Name & Relationship To The Parents

_____

_____

Message Or Advice For The Parents

_____

_____

_____

_____

_____

_____

Wishes For Baby

_____

_____

_____

_____

_____

_____

Predictions

Date Of Birth:	Time Of Birth:

Weight:	Height:	Hair & Eyes:	Name:

Guest

Name & Relationship To The Parents

_____

_____

Message Or Advice For The Parents

_____

_____

_____

_____

_____

Wishes For Baby

_____

_____

_____

_____

_____

Predictions

Date Of Birth:	Time Of Birth:

Weight:	Height:	Hair & Eyes:	Name:

Guest

Name & Relationship To The Parents

_____

_____

Message Or Advice For The Parents

_____

_____

_____

_____

_____

_____

Wishes For Baby

_____

_____

_____

_____

_____

_____

Predictions

	Date Of Birth:	Time Of Birth:
Weight:	Height:	Hair & Eyes:	Name:

Guest

Name & Relationship To The Parents

_____

_____

Message Or Advice For The Parents

_____

_____

_____

_____

_____

_____

Wishes For Baby

_____

_____

_____

_____

_____

_____

Predictions

Date Of Birth:

Time Of Birth:

Weight:

Height:

Hair & Eyes:

Name:

Guest

Name & Relationship To The Parents

_____

_____

Message Or Advice For The Parents

_____

_____

_____

_____

_____

Wishes For Baby

_____

_____

_____

_____

_____

Predictions

Date Of Birth:	Time Of Birth:

Weight:	Height:	Hair & Eyes:	Name:

Guest

Name & Relationship To The Parents

_____

_____

Message Or Advice For The Parents	Wishes For Baby
_____	_____
_____	_____
_____	_____
_____	_____
_____	_____

Predictions

Date Of Birth:	Time Of Birth:

Weight:	Height:	Hair & Eyes:	Name:

Guest

Name & Relationship To The Parents

_____

_____

Message Or Advice For The Parents

_____

_____

_____

_____

_____

Wishes For Baby

_____

_____

_____

_____

_____

Predictions

Date Of Birth:

Time Of Birth:

Weight:

Height:

Hair & Eyes:

Name:

Guest

Name & Relationship To The Parents

_____

_____

Message Or Advice For The Parents

_____

_____

_____

_____

_____

_____

Wishes For Baby

_____

_____

_____

_____

_____

Predictions

Date Of Birth:

Time Of Birth:

Weight:

Height:

Hair & Eyes:

Name:

Guest

Name & Relationship To The Parents

_____

_____

Message Or Advice For The Parents

_____

_____

_____

_____

_____

Wishes For Baby ♡

_____

_____

_____

_____

_____

Predictions

Date Of Birth:	Time Of Birth:

Weight:	Height:	Hair & Eyes:	Name:

Add Photos & Keepsakes

· Gift Log ·

Gift Log

Gift Received	Given By	Thank You Note Sent
		◯
		◯
		◯
		◯
		◯
		◯
		◯
		◯
		◯
		◯
		◯
		◯
		◯

Gift Log

Gift Received	Given By	Thank You Note Sent
		◯
		◯
		◯
		◯
		◯
		◯
		◯
		◯
		◯
		◯
		◯
		◯

Gift Log

Gift Received	Given By	Thank You Note Sent
_____	_____	◯
_____	_____	◯
_____	_____	◯
_____	_____	◯
_____	_____	◯
_____	_____	◯
_____	_____	◯
_____	_____	◯
_____	_____	◯
_____	_____	◯
_____	_____	◯
_____	_____	◯
_____	_____	◯

Gift Log

Gift Received	Given By	Thank You Note Sent
		◯
		◯
		◯
		◯
		◯
		◯
		◯
		◯
		◯
		◯
		◯
		◯

Gift Log

Gift Received	Given By	Thank You Note Sent
		◯
		◯
		◯
		◯
		◯
		◯
		◯
		◯
		◯
		◯
		◯
		◯
		◯

Gift Log

Gift Received	Given By	Thank You Note Sent
		◯
		◯
		◯
		◯
		◯
		◯
		◯
		◯
		◯
		◯
		◯
		◯

Gift Log

Gift Received	Given By	Thank You Note Sent
		○
		○
		○
		○
		○
		○
		○
		○
		○
		○
		○
		○
		○

Made in United States
Troutdale, OR
03/18/2025

29857666R00044